MW01100738

"Where does it say _ _ _ _ _ _ ?"

A Basic INDEX for

A COURSE IN MIRACLES

Indexing Miracles Group

SECTION I: BASIC WORDS & PHRASES
(ALPHABETIZED)

SECTION II: FOUR (4) TABLES OF CONTENTS
(ALPHABETIZED)

‡

keyed to
ORIGINAL EDITION
of
A COURSE IN MIRACLES
(1975, 1985)

plus
SECOND EDITION
of
A COURSE IN MIRACLES
(1992)

PREFACE

What is "A COURSE IN MIRACLES"?

Those who study the Course recognize early in the lessons that what they are actually learning is how to perceive in a new way. They must unlearn a system that is based on the belief in a physical reality, for the Course states that our only reality is Spirit, and our conflict comes from vacillating between the two thought systems.

One belief holds we are born into bodies for a short time - to experience some joy, some pain, some happiness, some grief, and eventually death.

The other belief - the Course's belief - is that we are created in our Creator's image, which is Spirit. In truth we are not bodies; we are extensions of the Thought of God. Although our natural inheritance is a state of love, we have chosen to dream that we have separated ourselves from our Source, and in so doing we think we have sinned. Based on that misperception comes all our guilt, and out of guilt comes fear. We can learn to release this fear and undo our mistaken sense of sin and guilt only through the practice of forgiveness, for it is by forgiving others that we learn to forgive ourselves, and thus our illusions of separation can be healed. As the Course states, "All healing involves replacing fear with love."

(Journey Without Distance, page 133)

"Forgiveness recognizes what you thought your brother did to you has not occurred. It does not pardon sins and make them real. It sees there was no sin."

(Workbook page 391/*401*)

The Course begins:

*"NOTHING REAL CAN BE THREATENED.
NOTHING UNREAL EXISTS.*

Herein lies the peace of God."

INTRODUCTION

Most *textbooks* have a "Contents" table at the beginning of the book, and an "Index" at the end. **"A COURSE IN MIRACLES"** has four Tables of Contents, but no "Index" as such.

This is a simplified **"INDEX"** to the COURSE, keyed to both the original published, (1975, 1985), and the Second Edition, (1992). It is a reference to many of the material words, phrases, and topics that have been studied over fifteen years since formal publication; that seem to repeatedly come up in informal discussion, as well as classes, by way of questions begging to be referenced to book and page of the COURSE.

Although each sentence of the COURSE shows the completeness of the COURSE itself, no such claim is made of this INDEX. It is a *guide* that is not a "concordance" in the true sense of the word. It is completely open-ended, yet at such a level as to be an *aid* to beginning as well as advanced students who choose to use it. It is with this thought in mind, (to be of *assistance* to those of us on our "journey without distance"), the INDEX is so constructed, and dedicated.

The case may be made that the COURSE is too vast, the language too complex, and the levels too varied to ever be simply cataloged by a "work" such as you hold in your hands now. And, the "case" would be entirely correct! However, the serious student/teacher has a gnawing inner "desire" to progress and learn more, and the INDEX has the purpose of *pointing* the reader in just that direction.

The four Tables of Contents have been alphabetized based on **key words** in Chapters, Subchapters, and Lessons subject headings. Even though there may be future revisions published, (of the first section of words/phrases, etc.), the student is encouraged to add to his/her own personal INDEX, in whatever way he/she may choose. When all is said and done, each of us has our own unique desk in the Holy Spirit's "classroom", at which we individualize our "learning" accordingly.

References to T, W, and M, stand for Text, Workbook, and Manual respectively. *(All page references pertaining to the* **SECOND EDITION** *of the COURSE are in* **ITALICS**.*)*

Liberty has been taken in numbering the pages in the "Preface" of the COURSE, since many words are clarified in that section. Parenthetical marks enclose the page numbers: (P-1), etc. (In the **Second Edition** the Preface pages are numbered in lower case Roman numerals.)

i

Also, several references have been made to Song of Prayer, and GOG, (Gifts of God), etc., pertaining to specific subjects. In SECTION II of the Index, (Workbook), the words **FORGIVENESS** and **LOVE** have been capitalized and highlighted wherever found.

KEY words are **HIGHLIGHTED** throughout the INDEX. The notations to these "keys" are either direct quotes, or direct allusions to quotes. These key words relate to specific descriptions of interest, although may not be included in the COURSE. These are enclosed in parenthesis, ( ), either to clarify, or to reference a subject that is not *directly* named in the page numbers indicated, or for which the *allusion* is described, or may be suggested, and is a continuing topic of discussion. Words such as "quantum physics", "symphonic arrangement", etc., have been mentioned so many times in discussions as *analogies* for processes in the COURSE, that they have been included as "key words". Where "keys" are mentioned more than two times, every effort has been made to alphabetize the subject pertaining to the keyed word. With one or two exceptions, where more than one page is indicated as a reference to the topic selected, the letter 'f' is inserted after the first page referenced, to indicated the *following page*, (and even *pages* in some cases), is applicable.

Where in the COURSE are these words mentioned? And **where** does "IT" talk about them, and all the many other phrases, expressions, etc., that are coming to have new meaning to all who are in the "classroom" of the Holy Spirit; words that will redefine one's "self" within the context of this new paradigm of understanding that is "A COURSE IN MIRACLES"?

There are students, teachers, of the COURSE that are walking storehouses of instant information, such as page numbers, and exact quotes, that frankly witness to the wonderful capacity of the Spirit-led brain and memory. One never ceases to be amazed at their *recall* that continually leads deeper into one's own study of any particular subject.

To those of us without such "recall" who would remember a word or subject, (and **where** same is found in "A COURSE IN MIRACLES", just a little bit faster, and more completely), it is hoped the INDEX will be of assistance.

ADDITIONS / NOTES

SECTION I :
WORDS AND PHRASES
ALPHABETICAL

Page / *Page*

A

ABILITIES T-37,94,110,437; M-59
T-41,102,118,470; M-62

ABRUPTLY lifted up and hurled into reality T-322
T-346

ABSTRACT; ABSTRACTIONS T-51;W-297;M-67
T-56;W-304;M-70

ABUNDANCE (vs scarcity) T-9,120; W-408
T-11,130; W-418

What could you not **ACCEPT** W-247
W-255

ACCEPTING the Atonement for yourself T-555
T-598

No **ACCIDENTS** in Salvation M-6
M-7

The role of the **ACCUSER** T-613
T-659

ADAM (sleep) ....(P-4); T-14f
(xi); T-17f

You will **ADVANCE** T-353
T-378

ADVANCED teachers of God M-8
M-9

ADVANCES (vs retreats...learning ACIM) T-357
T-383

AFRAID of God (fear your brother) T-393
T-421f

AGREED to meet (reunion) M-4
M-5

ALIEN W-331
W-339

God cannot destroy the **ALIEN** will T-554
T-597

ALL are called, few choose to listen ....T-39,(T-59,398;W-278)
T-44,(T-65,427;W-285)

ALTAR T-36,86,510; W-346; M-82
T-41,93,548; W-355; M-86

"ALWAYS" (can not understand it...has no direction)................T-221f
T-237f

Second Edition numbers in *italics*

ADDITIONS / NOTES

Love...**AMBIVALENCE** (simultaneous conflicting feelings) T-55
T-61

The great **AMNESIA** T-392
T-420

AMONG the Ministers of God W-281
W-288

ANALYZE (the ego) T-274
T-295

ANCIENT hatred...present love T-522,592
T-562,637

ANCIENT journey (end of) T-366
T-393

ANGELS T-522; W-478
T-562; W-488

ANGER T-84,297
T-91,319

ANGER (never justified) T-85,593
T-92,638

A slight twinge of **ANNOYANCE** W-32
W-32

ANOTHER can be found ....(T-295); W-319
(T-317); W-327

God's **ANSWER** given (to idea of separation) T-515; M-4
T-554; M-5

ANTI-CHRIST T-575f
T-619f

ANXIETY T-57
T-62

(**ANXIETY** attack) ....(T-436)
(T-468)

APOCALYPSE T-30
T-34

APPEAL (for love; help; healing) T-200f
T-215f

APPEARANCES T-589-599
T-634-644

APPRECIATION (appropriate response to your brother) T-201
T-216

ARK of peace (entered two by two) T-404
T-433

ARK of safety T-561f
T-604f

ARROGANCE T389; W-343
T-417; W-352

ASK ("consider"), "what is it for?" T-16,341,479
T-19,366,515

Second Edition numbers in *italics*

ADDITIONS / NOTES

Dreams...in a mind **ASLEEP**...T-574
                                                                              T-618
...joined as one...**ASUNDER** T-332
                                                                              T-356
Accept **ATONEMENT** for yourself T-555
                                                                              T-598
ATONEMENT (final miracle; escape past) T-19; M-58
                                                                              T-23; M-61
ATONEMENT principle T-2f,8; M-46
                                                                              T-4f,9; M-48
ATONEMENT (set into motion) T-1,6,16; M-85
                                                                              T-3,8,19; M-89
ATTACK T-450,569
                                                                              T-483,612
ATTACK-defense (cycle) W-277
                                                                              W-284
ATTITUDES are ego-based T-52
                                                                              T-57
ATTRACTION(S)...of guilt T-382
                                                                              T-410
        ...of pain T-386
                                                                              T-414
        ...of death T-388
                                                                              T-416
AUTHORITY "problem" T-43f
                                                                              T-48f
AUTHORSHIP T-43
                                                                              T-48
(AVATARS) ....(M-2,61)
                                                                              (M-2,64)
(A)-WAKE (gentle; not frighten) T-96,542; W-313
                                                                              T-104,584f; W-321
AWAKEN and return to me (peace at last) T-35,238;W-445
                                                                              T-39,255;W-455
AWAKING unto Christ T-236
                                                                              T-253
AWE (vs fear) T-3,5,13
                                                                              T-5,7,16

B

BARGAINS T-421
                                                                              T-451
(BE)-CAUSE T-432
                                                                              T-463

Second Edition numbers in *italics*

ADDITIONS / NOTES

Our **BEHAVIOR** T-612
          T-658

BEHOLD me brother, at your hand I die T-526
          T-566

BE still T-602; W-350
          T-648; W-360

BELIEF is an ego function T-52
          T-57

BELIEVED entirely or not at all (ACIM) T-440
          T-473

BIBLE (errors) T-36,80,87
          T-40,87,95

BIRTH not beginning; death not end M-58
          M-61

BIRTH of fear (conflict) T-454
          T-488

BIRTHPLACE of guilt M-43
          M-45

BITTER idols M-84
          M-88

BLAME T-187
          T-201

The **BLIND** T-416
          T-446

BODY, What is ? T-12,140,479,543; W-415
          T-15,151,515,585; W-425

BODY T-38,217,364,367,410,
          T-43,233,390,394,440,

BODY T-412,566f; W-122
          T-442,609f; W-124

BODY (to deny...a learning device) T-20f
          T-24f

BODY (should not feel at all) W-252
          W-260

BODY (God did not make) T-97
          T-105

BODY is neutral T-559
          T-602

BODY does nothing...is meaningless T-389
          T-418

BODY (as a sign of life) T-527
          T-567

BORN again T-234,603
          T-251,648

In this learning is Salvation **BORN** T-614
          T-660

Page 4

Second Edition numbers in *italics*

ADDITIONS / NOTES

BRAIN T-436
                                          T-468

BRIDGE T-321; W-243
                                    T-345; W-249

My BURDEN light (My message is Light) T-71
                                          T-77

BUSY doing on which you are sent T-364
                                          T-390

C

All are CALLED, few choose to listen ....T-39,(T-59,350; M-33)
                                  T-44,(T-65,375; M-34)

You have been CALLED T-350
                                          T-375

The ritual of completion (CANNIBALISM) T-319
                                          T-343

CARPET of Time ... ("threads" T-622) ....T-221,(348),(353)
                ("   T-668)   *T-237,(373),(378)*

CATHOLIC reasoning T-520
                                          T-560

CAUSE/Effect T-19f,27,420,517,550
                             T-23f,31,450,556,592

Course in CAUSE, not Effect T-432
                                          T-463

Reversing CAUSE & Effect T-550f
                                          T-592f

CELESTIAL order T-3
                                          T-5

Quiet CENTER T-363
                                          T-390

CENTRAL Theme (of ACIM) M-3
                                          M-3

CENTURY of contemplation T-363
                                          T-389f

CHAIN of special relationships...of savagery T-295
                                          T-317f

CHANGE your mind T-415
                                          T-445

(3 steps) to CHANGE your thoughts W-34
                                          W-34

Where...no meaning, there is CHAOS T-415
                                          T-445

CHARITY T-23
                                          T-27

Second Edition numbers in *italics*

ADDITIONS / NOTES

CHILD in you W-331
W-339

My brother, **CHOOSE** again ....T-619f; (PSYCH)-20
T-666f;   "   "

You **CHOOSE** your dreams T-574
T-618

CHOSEN ones T-39; W-278; M-3
T-44;W-285; M-3

CHRIST, What is ? W-421
W-431

CHRISTIAN in statement, (the terminology) ....(P-2)
(ix)

CHRISTMAS T-304
T-327

The **CHURCHES** it builds to itself T-238
T-256

CIM (believed entirely, or not at all) T-440
T-473

CIRCLE of creation T-550
T-593

CIRCLE of fear T-367
T-394

CIRCULARITY (forms of) T-544
T-587

CLAIM God's answer W-121
W-122

CO-CREATOR T-585
T-630

(Against **CO-DEPENDENCY**) T-58,493
T-63f,530

(**CODEPENDENCY**) (recovery from) T-564
T-607

Everyone is (**CO-DEPENDENT**) T-79,98,318
T-86,106,342

COLLABORATIVE venture T-63
T-69

There will **COME** a time T-613
T-660

COMMITMENT T-34
T-38

COMMUNION is another kind of completion T-384
T-412

COMPANIONS...holy; mighty T-222; M-10
T-238, M-11

COMPARISON... an ego device T-466
T-502

Page 6

ADDITIONS / NOTES

COMPETITIVE T-559
    T-602

COMPLEXITY is of the ego T-289
    T-310

COMPROMISE T-460
    T-495

When every **CONCEPT**...raised to doubt T-610-14
    T-656-60

CONCRETE T-51,63;W-297;M-51
    T-56,69;W-304;M-53

CONFLICT (meaningless; root of all evil)...(cp. T-43) .T-115,184,452f
    T-124,199,486f

Transition and period of **CONFUSION** T-211,322
    T-226,346

CONSCIOUSNESS (induces action; ego domain) T-5,37
    T-7,42

CONSTANCY arises T-614
    T-661

Any decision affects a **CONSTELLATION** T-257
    T-276

CONTEMPLATION (your way will be different) T-363
    T-389f

(Form vs) **CONTENT** T-458f
    T-493f

Your **CONTRIBUTION**...disproportionate T-356
    T-382

CORRECTION of your brother (for all who cannot see) T-155f,212
    T-166f,228

Forget this **COURSE** W-350
    W-360

COURSE (believed entirely or not at all) T-440
    T-473

COURSE in cause and not effect T-432
    T-463

COURSE in mind training...(cp. WB-69) T-13
    (cp.WB-69)   *T-16*

COURSE is easy...(but very difficult...W-77) T-460
    "   *T-495*

COURSE is your language T-437
    T-469

COURSE on how to know yourself T-312
    T-335

COURSE on miracles T-389
    T-418

(**COVENANT**) (birth of the Son ..."Promise") T-404,560
    T-433,603

ADDITIONS / NOTES

Impossible to **CREATE** (vs Make) T-23,39,44,333,390
                                       T-27,44,49,358,418
CREATION, What is ? T-14,63,480,516,560; W-451
                          T-17,69,516,556,603; W-461
Your **CREATIONS** T-104
                             T-112
CRUCIAL period in this Course T-440
                             T-472
CRUCIFIXION (last "useless journey") T-47
                             T-52
CRUCIFIXION (Jesus never "suffered pain") T-87,526
                             T-94,566
"CURE" W-263
                             W-270
CURRICULUM: ACIM (vs ego's) T-210f
                             T-226f

D

The **DARK** ones...the army of the powerless...a sorry army T-430f
                             T-462
DEATH ... it will not work; the central dream T-97;M-63
                             T-104;M-66
DEATH penalty T-216
                             T-232
There is no **DEATH** T-9,529,575
                             T-11,569,619
In **DEATH** is sin preserved T-607
                             T-652
...not **DEBATABLE** (your Worth) T-49
                             T-54
DECIDE for me (my role; part; strength) T-258; W-99,121,281
                             T-278; W-101,122,288
DECISION (continuous) T-464,581
                             T-499,625
DEDICATION (to death...to life) T-389f
                             T-417f
DEFENSES T-15f; W-250f; M-12
                             T-19f; W-257f; M-14
DEFENSES do...**DEFEND** T-334
                             T-359
DEMONSTRATE (to teach; constant process...sleeping) M-1
                             M-1
DENIAL (Process of...M-43) T-59,118,202,539; W-250
       ("   M-45)   *T-65,127,217,581; W-257*

Second Edition numbers in *italics*

ADDITIONS / NOTES

DENY the denial of truth T-203
                                          T-218
DEPRESSION T-.57,140,211,511,526,569, 617; W-63,120
                       T-63,155,227,550,567,613,663; W-63,121f
DESIRE T-353; M-23
                                      T-379; M-24
DESPAIR T-219
                                      T-235
DETOUR into fear T-14
                                      T-17
DEVIL ("great deceiver" T-427)...("accuser" T-613) T-44f
     ("   "   T-458)...("   T-659)   *T-49f*
DEVOTION to a brother T-47
                                      T-52
DIED in vain (teach not that I...) T-193
                                      T-209
DIFFERENCES are of the body T-435
                                      T-467
DIFFERENCE/Sameness M-5
                                      M-6
DIRECT (guide, lead) W-99
                                      W-101
DISASTER is not real T-311
                                      T-334
DISOBEYING God's Will (...impossible) T-123
                                      T-133
DISSOCIATION T-215
                                      T-231
DOING this unto yourself T-545
                                      T-587
...being **DONE** to me T-545
                                      T-587
(When in **DOUBT** what I should do) T-256f,341,348
                               T-275f,366,373
DREAM (s)...T-577f
                                      T-622f
DREAMER of the world of dreams T-542
                                      T-584
DREAMING...of the world T-543
                                      T-585
DREAMS (sleeping/waking) T-350f,542,597
                               T-375f,584,642
       Happy T-352
                                      T-377f
       perceptual temper tantrums T-350
                                      T-376

Second Edition numbers in *italics*

ADDITIONS / NOTES

"**DYNAMICS**" of the ego T-317
                                                   T-341

E

Attempt to fly ...**EAGLE** M-8
                                                   M-9

EASTER T-394; W-273
                                           T-423; W-280

EASTER (poem in Gifts of God) ....GOG
                                           GOG

EFFECT and cause (split off...reversed) T-552
                                           T-594

EGO, What is? T-61,117,121; W-120,457
                               T-67,126,130f; W-121,467

EGO always speaks first T-80,92
                                           T-87,100

EGO enjoys studying itself T274
                                           T-295

EGO identification T-206
                                         T-221f

EGO is insane T-457; W-78
                                     T-491f; W-78

EGO is legion T-91
                                           T-99

EGO never occurred T-90
                                           T-98

EGO plan for Salvation T-157,542; W-120
                                   T-169,584; W-121

EGO wants your death T-216
                                         T-232

EGO (the world of...equals nothing) T-117
                                         T-126

The ("**ELECT**") T-502
                                         T-540

One **EMOTION** that you made T-437
                                         T-469

The only **EMOTIONS** (fear and love) T-202
                                         T-217

EMPTINESS engendered by fear T-9
                                          T-11

Holy **ENCOUNTER** T-132
                                         T-142

All will have an **END** T-572
                                         T-616

Page 10

Second Edition numbers in *italics*

ADDITIONS / NOTES

ENGINE of destruction (the body) T-412
T-442

ERROR (sin vs error) T-374f
T-402f

ETERNITY T-105,544
T-113,586

EVOLUTION T-17
T-20

Only an **EXPERIENCE** M-73
M-77

EXTEND T-14; W-47
T-17; W-47

EYES T-442f
T-474f

F

FACE of innocence ...wet with tears T-610f
T-656f

FACTS T-516
T-555

FADE away (effects) T-553; M-5
T-596; M-6

(OK to **"FAIL"**, now) ....(W-237)
(W-243)

FAIRY tales T-159
T-170

FAITH (ask) T-338,343,373
T-363,368,400

Little **FAITH** T-497
T-534

The **"FALL"** (the "separation") T-11,45
T-13,50

FANTASY T-12,159,316; W-34
T-12,170,339; W-34

FATHERHOOD T-104f,550
T-112f,592

FEAR (the call for help...for love) T-202,225,538,617
T-217,242,580,664

FEAR of God (be not afraid to look) T-391,563; W-346
T-420,606; W-355

FEAR is judgment T-11,579
T-13,624

FEAR ...one emotion that you made T-437
T-469

ADDITIONS / NOTES

Nothing to **FEAR** T-563; W-99
    T-606; W-100
How do you **FEEL**? T-460
    T-494
FEET still touching earth T-591
    T-636
FINAL step ....(P-6); T-591
    (xiii); T-636
(**FIRST** 35 years) ....(T-610)
    (T-657)
FIRST Cause T-259
    T-279
FLY (sparrow...eagle) M-8
    M-9
FOLLOWING Him is the easiest thing in the world T-126
    T-136
FOOLISH thing T-308
    T-331
a **FORCE**..T-446
    T-479
FOREVER always T-218
    T-234
FORGET this course ....(T-602); W-350
    (T-648); W-360
God does not **FORGIVE** W-99
    W-100
FORGIVENESS: (3-step process) T-83; W-34,118,365
    T-90; W-34,119,375
    What is? ....(P-6); T-41,156,493; W-34,99,213,242f,391
        (xiii); T-46,168,530; W-34,100,217,248f,401
    What it is not (to destroy) ....(P-6); T-528
        (xiii); T-568
    to destroy ....(T-528,593); Song of Pr.
        (T-568,638); Song of Pr.
    offers everything I want T-41,373; W-145,213
        T-46,400; W-147,217
    false T-594
        T-638
    of myself..T-526
        T-566
    for what he has not done T-256,330,590
        T-275f,354,635
FORGOTTEN Song T-415f
    T-445f
FORM (vs content) T-458f,506; M-3,64
    T-493f,544; M-3,67

Second Edition numbers in *italics*

ADDITIONS / NOTES

FORMS T-506,523; M-73
T-544,563; M-77
FRAGMENTED T-347
T-372
FREE will ....T-(Introd.),14; M-75
T-(Introd.),17; M-79
FRIEND T-585
T-629
FUNCTION T-214,259f,493; W-342
T-230,279f,529; W-351

G

GAME of guilt is played T-523
T-563
GAP T-554,563
T-597,606
GARDEN of Eden T-14,33
T-17,37
GATES of hell T-469
T-505
GENERALIZATION (process) T-213
T-229
GENTLENESS (power; strength; might) T-264,488;M-11
T-284;525;M-12
GIVING is the proof of having T-567
T-611
GIVING and receiving T-96,154
T-104,165f
GIVING (must return...be more) W-345
W-354
GLORY T-451
T-485
Our only **GOAL** T-13
T-15
GOD cannot destroy the alien will T-554
T-597
GOD (doesn't see; knows not) T-34; W-251
T-38; W-258
GOD dwells within T-574
T-618
GOD Is (Father by His Son) T-550; W315
T-592; W-323
GOD is not a body T-361
T-387

Page 13

ADDITIONS / NOTES

And **GOD** thinks otherwise T-452
T-486
You are **GOD** T-5,74,312
T-7,81,336
GOD'S meaning (your meaning) T-108
T-116
GOLDEN Rule T-7,11
T-10,13
"**GOOD**" T-520
T-560
GOSSIP T-382
T-410
GRACE T-33,126f,373f; W-315
T-37,136f,401; W-323
GRATITUDE T-3; W-362,367
T-5; W-372,377
GREAT Rays T-175,299,321f,354; W-474
T-189,322,345f,380; W-484
GRIEF T-526
T-566
(**GROUP** studying dynamic) leaders T-603
T-648f
GUILT demands punishment T-77,455,515
T-84,490,554
GUILT has driven you insane T-220
T-236
GUILT implies it, (the separation), was accomplished T-348
T-373
Remember, *you* made **GUILT** T-356
T-382
The game of **GUILT** is played T-523
T-563
GUILTLESS are **GUILTY** T-224
T-240

H

HABIT of response T-606
T-651
HALLUCINATION(S) T-413f
T-443f
Everything...**HAPPENED**...never **HAPPENED** T-356
T-382
...prefer to be right or **HAPPY**? T-573
T-617

Second Edition numbers in *italics*

ADDITIONS / NOTES

HAPPY dreams (**HAPPINESS**...T-433f) T-357,542,573,598
       ("   *T-465f*)   *T-382,584,617,643*
HAPPY learner (happy lightheartedness) T-252f; M-9
                                    T-272f; M10
HATE *is* an illusion T-314
                                      T-338
HAVING and being T-67,182,516
                                 T-73,197,556
HEAL one (heal all) T-517
                                      T-557
To **HEAL** is to make whole T-595
                                      T-640
HEALING (not a miracle ... process) T-19,35
                                      T-23,39
HEALING is release from the past T-240
                                      T-258
HEALTH (inner peace) T-15,146
                                      T-18,157
HEAR the HS T-57
                                      T-62
HEAVEN T-35,213,271,349,359,369,425; M-56,58
              T-39,229,292,374,384,396,455; M-59,61
Until you choose **HEAVEN**, you are in Hell T-440
                                      T-473
HELL T-280; W-331; M-2
                                  T-301; W-339; M-2
Fear is **HELL** ("**HELL-fire**" concept T-9) T-617
       ("   "   *T-12*)   *T-664*
"HELP" a brother T-201
                                      T-216
HERE ... there T-533,591
                                    T-574f,635
HERO of the dream T-543; W-339
                                    T-585; W-348
HIERARCHY of illusions T-515
                                      T-554
HISTORY T-51
                                      T-56
(**HITLER, HUSSEIN**) ....(T-543)
                                    (T-585f)
HOLIEST of all the spots on earth T-522
                                      T-562
HOLINESS is positive T-410
                                      T-440
(**HOLOGRAM**) ....(T-417; W-451)
                                 (T-447; W-461)

Second Edition numbers in *italics*

ADDITIONS / NOTES

HOLY ENCOUNTER T-132,618; M-6
                                                                      T-142,664; M-7
HOLY ground T-349
                                                                      T-374
HOLY INSTANT T-325,419
                                                                      T-349,450
HOLY RELATIONSHIP T-337,363; M-6
                                                                      T-362,389; M-7
HOLY SPIRIT, What is? T-67; W-427
                                                                      T-73; W-437
HOLY TRINITY T-35
                                                                      T-39
HONEST; willing; open (triangle) T-583
                                                                      T-627
No one who comes...still have **HOPE** T-573
                                                                      T-617
HOPE ... HOPELESSNESS T-484
                                                                      T-521
HORIZONTAL (vs vertical) T-5f
                                                                      T-7f
HOST of God T-360
                                                                      T-386
HOW do you feel? T-460
                                                                      T-494
HOW do you make the choice? T-620
                                                                      T-666
HUMILITY T-308,355; W-101
                                                                      T-331,381;W-102
...abruptly lifted up and **HURLED** into reality..............................T-322
                                                                      T-346
HURT or be hurt T-88
                                                                      T-96

I

I, What am ? W-469
                                                                      W-479
I AM as God created me T-620; W-162,195,300
                                                                      T-667; W-164,199,307
I am here only to be truly helpful T-24
                                                                      T-28
I am safe T-150
                                                                      T-161
I do not know T-614
                                                                      T-660

ADDITIONS / NOTES

Second Edition numbers in *italics*

ADDITIONS / NOTES

JESUS (in charge of Atonement...Second Coming) T-6,58f
T-8,64f
JESUS ("I am incomplete...") W-322
W-330
JESUS (difference...now...I have nothing else) T-5
T-7
JESUS (did not "suffer pain")...T-526f,560
T-566f,603
JOIN ... JOINING (...minds) ....(P-5)
(xii)
JOURNEY beyond words W-328
W-336
JOURNEY that is done W-316
W-324
JOURNEY (last useless....meaningless) T-47,239,354
T-52,257,380
JOURNEY without distance T-139,366
T-150,393
JOY T-66; W-177; M-12
T-72; W-180; M-13
JUDAS T-87
T-95
JUDGMENT (condemnation):
  give you false direction T-415
T-446
  impossible M-26
M-27
  is not your function T-216
T-232
  one right use of T-58
T-64
  taught yourself...a toy...no value T-410f
T-440f
  makes you tired T-42
T-47

K

KINGDOM of God ... Heaven T-54,63,358
T-60,69,384
Impossible to **KNOW** T-40
T-45
Course in how to **KNOW** yourself T-312
T-335
I do not **KNOW** T-277,614
T-298,660

Second Edition numbers in *italics*

ADDITIONS / NOTES

KNOWING is not open to interpretation T-40
    T-45
KNOWLEDGE T-41
    T-46
KNOWLEDGE (goal) T-128
    T-138
Son...**KNOWS** everything his Father understands T-591
    T-636

L

LACK ("scarcity principle") T-11
    T-13
LADDER T-357
    T-383
your **LANGUAGE** (ACIM) T-437
    T-469
LAST JUDGMENT, What is ? T-30,508f; W-445
    T-35,547; W-455
LAST step T-379; W-388; M-65
    T-407; W-398; M-68
Don't **LAUGH** at someone else, or your self T-42
    T-47
Your **LAUGHTER** and your brother's joined T-545
    T-587
LAWS of God (Spirit) T-120,403; W132
    T-129f,432; W-134
LAWS of man (ego) W-132
    W-134
LEADERS T-603
    T-649
Don't say "I cant **LEARN** it" T-437,442; M-36
    T-469,474f; M-37
LEARNING (has occurred...is invisible) T-213
    T-229
LEARNING model (is all...change) T-71,84,606
    T-77f,91,652
LEGIONS upon legions W-255
    W-262
LESSON plans T-611
    T-657
LET Holy Spirit undo T-83
    T-90
LEVEL confusion T-19,455
    T-23,489

ADDITIONS / NOTES

LEVEL of communication T-20
                                         T-24

LIFE T-459
                                         T-493f

Quiet **LIGHT** T-213
                                         T-228

Happy **LIGHTHEARTEDNESS** M-9
                                         M-10

LITTLE faith T-497
                                         T-534f

LITTLE willingness (perfect W's T-205) T-354
             ("   " T-220)   *T-380*

Learning ...world is **LOOSENING** its grasp T-613
                                         T-659

("**LORD'S** Prayer") (...wander into temptation...) ....(T-326)
                                        (T-350)

Voice...**LOUD** as...willingness to listen T-145
                                         T-157

LOVE ("at first sight" concept) ....(T-436f)
                                       (T-468f)

LOVE ...casts out fear T-12
                                         T-14

LOVE is content, and not form T-319
                                       T-343

LOVE is extension...offers everything forever T-464
                                       T-499

LOVE (first defined) ....(P-5); T-3
                                  (xi); T-5

LOVE (LOVE vs love) T-317
                                       T-341

LOVE (description of "in love") ....(T-411)
                                     (T-441)

LOVE ...never in world of dreams T-554
                                       T-597f

LOVE ...not an illusion...a fact T-314
                                       T-338

M

You **MADE** the world you see T-420
                                       T-450

MAGIC ("cure") T-2,19f; W-263
                              T-4,23f; W-270

MAKE (vs create) T-23,39,44,333
                              T-27,44,49,357f

Second Edition numbers in *italics*

ADDITIONS / NOTES

MAKE the error real T-205
                                                   T-221

MAKING over creation, the victory T-390
                                                   T-418

MARK of God T-4,50
                                                   T-6,56

("modern" **MARRIAGE**) ....(T-435)
                                                 (T-467)

lifelong (**MARRIAGE**) ....(M-7)
                                                  (M-8)

...not call for **MARTYRS**, but for teachers T-88
                                                 T-95

MEANS (vs way) T-548
                                                   T-590

MEDIATOR between two worlds T-238
                                                   T-256

MEDICATIONS T-20f
                                                   T-24f

(**MEDITATION**) "Be still..." W-350
                                                   W-360

MEEK shall inherit the earth T-50
                                                   T-56

All will **MEET** again M-7
                                                   M-8

MEMORY (remembering) T-547f
                                                   T-589f

MESSAGES ... MESSENGER T-436,444
                                                 T-468,477

MIGHTY changes...quickly brought about T-590
                                                   T-634

MIGHTY companions M-10
                                                   M-11

MILLIONS of years T-30; M-4
                                               T-34; M-5

MIND ("change") T-27,359f; W-236
                                       T-31,385f; W-242

   how to direct W-477
                                                   W-487

   the mechanism of decision T-207
                                                   T-223

   the power of T-517
                                                   T-556

   wandering, (too tolerant of) T-25
                                                   T-29

  Course in **MIND** training T-13
                                                   T-16

ADDITIONS / NOTES

I am among the **MINISTERS** of God W-281
W-288
MIRACLE, What is ? T-1f,19,214,598; W-463
T-3f,23,230,642f; W473
MIRACLE does nothing...undo T-547
T-589
MIRACLE workers T-65
T-71
MIRROR (principal) T-477,483,570,617
T-513,519,614,664
MISCREATE T-28,34
T-32,39
MISSION (His...Your) T-209
T-224
MISTAKE (error, vs sin) T-375f
T-402f
(MONEY) ....(W-132)
(W-134)
MONEY, ($), (food), things T-238f,543; W-79
T-256f,585; W-79
The **"MORE**-than-everything"** T-576f; W-285
T-620f; W-293
MOTIVATION for learning this course T-128
T-138
Move **MOUNTAINS** T-27
T-31
Frightened **MOUSE** T-431,446
T-462,479
MURDER T-460f
T-495f
MYSTERIES T-157
T-169
MYTHS (perceptual...fearful...and magic) T-53
T-58f

N

I **NEED** do nothing T-200,362,549f
T-215,388,591f
NEEDS T-11,547
T-13,589
Body is **NEUTRAL** T-559
T-602
No **NEUTRAL** things W-28
W-28

Second Edition numbers in *italics*

ADDITIONS / NOTES

No **NEUTRAL** thoughts W-26
W-26
Time is **NEUTRAL** T-519
T-559
NIGHTMARE T-2f
T-4f
Blackest **NIGHTMARES** T-249
T-268
Not one **NOTE** in Heaven's song was missed T-512
T-550
NOTHING (nuances) T-28,253,348,360,453,495,597
T-32,272,373,386,487,532,642
NOW T-603; M-45
T-648; M-47

O

OBSTACLES to peace T-379
T-406
"Be" **ONE** T-35
T-39
ONENESS W-315
W-323
World ...**OPPOSITE** of Heaven T-317
T-341
(OUT-OF-BODY) experience ....(T-361)
(T-387)
Nothing **OUTSIDE** you T-358
T-384
OVERLOOK T-568
T-611
OWNERSHIP is a dangerous concept T-238
T-256

P

PAIN T-386,591; W-351
T-414,635; W-361
PAIN (vs pleasure) T-386,537f
T -414,579f
(PARADIGM) shift T-472, 613f
T-508,659f
PARDON...to overlook the "truth" W-242f
W-248f
Forget the **PAST** T-547
T-598

Page 23

ADDITIONS / NOTES

There is no **PAST**; is gone T-221,323f
    T-237,347f
Infinite **PATIENCE** T-81
    T-88
PEACE of God T-91,238; W-339
    T-99,255; W-348
PERCEPTION (into knowledge...the transfer process) T-213; W-67
    T-229; W-67
PERCEPTION (see PROJECTION)...has never been ....(P-4); T-219
    (xii); T-235
PERCEPTION'S law T-612
    T-658
("**PERFECT** person") ....(T-291)
    (T-313)
PERIOD of confusion...of disorientation T-322
    T-346
"**PERIOD(S)**"...(in the development of trust) M-8f
    M-10f
PICTURE of crucifixion T-525
    T-565
PICTURE (frame) T-485
    T-521f
Two **PICTURES** T-333
    T-357
(**PILLS**) ....(T-20; W-132)
    (T-24; W-134)
PITY T-528
    T-568
PLACE of safety T-461; W-76
    T-496; W-76
Everything...gently **PLANNED** W-247
    W-255
PLANNING T-519; W-245
    T-559; W-252
Not a **PLAY** on words T-442
    T-474
PLEASURE T-527
    T-567
POVERTY is lack...is of the ego T-205f
    T-220f
POWER T-531
    T-572
PRAYER T-1,40,152; M-51
    T-3,46,163; M-53
The Great **PREOCCUPATION** (the concept of the self) T-613
    T-659

Second Edition numbers in *italics*

ADDITIONS / NOTES

The **PRESENT** T-618
                        T-665
PRIDE T-167
                        T-179
PRISONERS T-401
                        T-431
PROBLEMS T-536f
                        T-578f
PRODIGAL son T-138
                        T-148f
PROGRAM (organized, well-structured...carefully planned) T-205
                        T-220
PROJECTION makes Perception ....(P-4);T-14,89,120,415,
                     (xii); T-17,96,129,445,
                      ....T-545; M-43
                      T-587; M-45
(The **"PROMISE"**) ....(T-404)
                        (T-433f)
PSYCHOTHERAPY ... PSYCHOTHERAPIST T-159
                        T-171
PUNISHMENT T-376
                        T-404
PURIFICATION T-1,75,296
                        T-3,82,318
PURIFICATION is of God T-356
                        T-381

Q

(**QUANTUM** physics) ....(T-141)
                        (T-152)
Best **QUESTION** you could ask T-51
                        T-56
Vague, unanswered **QUESTION** T-457
                        T-491
Willingness to **QUESTION** every value T-464; W-140
                        T-499; W-142
Your **QUESTIONS** have no answer M-78
                        M-82
QUESTIONS (only the ego...answers) T-37,274,426,
                        T-42,295,457,
                      ....T-533f; M-73,77
                      T-575f; M-77,81
QUIET center T-364
                        T-390

ADDITIONS / NOTES

QUIET Light T-213
                                                                    T-228

R

Great **RAYS** T-175,299,321f,354; W-474
                                    T-189,322,345f,380; W-484
READINESS is not mastery T-29; M-14
                                                              T-33; M-15
REAL WORLD, What is? T-236f,573,579,590; W-433
                                    T-254f,617,623,635; W-443
REALITY T-589,597
                                                                T-634,642
REALIZE ("REAL-EYES") T-611
                                                                    T-657
REASON T-434f
                                                                    T-465f
The sick have **REASON** for...unnatural desires...strange needs..... T-526
                                                                    T-567
REASONING by which the world is made T-540
                                                                    T-582
REBIRTH... dawning on your mind T-86
                                                                    T-93
REDEEMED T-218
                                                                    T-234
REINCARNATION .... (T-512,543f,572f); M-57
                                    (T-551f,585f,616f); M-60
There is no order in **RELATIONSHIPS** T-408
                                                                    T-437
"**RELIGIONS**".. W-133
                                                                    W-135
REQUEST T-40,55,151; W-462
                                    T-45,61,162; W-472
RESURRECTION T-539; M-65
                                                              T-581; M-68
REVELATION (highly personal...experience...
          ...indescribable...unutterable ...)...................... T-1,3f,67
                                                              T-3,5f,73
The great **REVERSAL** T-458
                                                                    T-492f
...prefer to be **RIGHT** or happy T-573,583
                                                                T-617,627
RIGHT (vs wrong) T-583
                                                                    T-627
RING of fear T-367
                                                                    T-394

Second Edition numbers in *italics*

ADDITIONS / NOTES

RISK in thinking death is peace T-541
                    T-583

ROCK of truth...on which salvation rests T-497
                    T-534

Behold your **ROLE** T-617
                    T-664

"The **ROOT** of all evil" (the authority problem) T-43
                    T-48

RULES for decision T-581f
                    T-625f

S

SACRIFICE (idea so mad) T-302f,574,596f; W-345f; M-32f
         T-325f,618,641f; W-354f; M-33f

You are **SAFE**; I am **SAFE** T-317; W-150
               T-340; W-152

SALVATION, What is? (a collaborative venture) T-63; W-397
               T-69; W-426

        (...is easy) T-356
                    T-382

        (a game) W-278
                   W-286

        (a paradox) T-590
                    T-635

        (...is simple) T-304
                    T-326

        (...is undoing) T-614
                    T-660

SALVATION'S song T-621
                    T-668

SAME (vs different) M-5
                    M-6

Whoever is **SANER** T-358
                    T-384

SAVE the world W-244
                    W-250

SAVING time T-363
                    T-389

SAVIORS of the world T-620
                    T-667

SCARCITY (lack) T-9,11,52,238,573f
           T-11,13,58,256,617f

SCRIPTS T-596f
                    T-640f

SECOND COMING, What is? T-58,158f; W-439,445
          T-64,170; W-449,455

ADDITIONS / NOTES

SECRECY T-436f
                                              T-469

SECRET of Salvation...doing this unto yourself T-545
                                              T-587

SECRET vow...**SECRET** oath T-560
                                              T-603

SEE...your brother...dream your Father T-543
                                              T-585

SEEING can but represent a wish T-618
                                              T-665

SEEK, but do not find T-208,318; W-120
                                    T-223,342; W-121

SEEK not to change the world T-415
                                              T-445

SEEMING T-108
                                              T-117

SELF-DECEPTION W-243
                                              W-249

SELF-ESTEEM (the way to build it) T-486
                                              T-523

SELF-FULLNESS (vs) **SELFISHNESS** T-122f
                                            T-132f

Cannot **SELL** your soul T-212
                                              T-227

SENSELESS musings W-261
                                              W-268

SEPARATION T-320
                                              T-344

SEPARATION occurred over millions of years T-30
                                              T-34

SERENITY T-109
                                              T-117

SHATTERED T-348f
                                              T-373f

SHORTEN suffering T-23
                                              T-27

SHOULD(S) T-569
                                              T-613

...agrees to be **SICK** T-553
                                              T-596

The **SICK** are merciless T-526
                                              T-566

SICKNESS is anger taken out upon the body.................T-560
                                              T-603

All **SICKNESS** comes from separation...defense..............T-514; W-250
                                      T-554; W-257

Second Edition numbers in *italics*

ADDITIONS / NOTES

Page 29

Second Edition numbers in *italics*

ADDITIONS / NOTES

SPECIAL hate/love relationship T-313f
                                        T-337f
SPECIALNESS T-477f
                                        T-513f
SPECIFIC T-340f
                                        T-366
SPIRIT is will T-209
                                        T-225
Your **SPIRIT** T-49
                                        T-54
(**SPIRITUAL** awakening) ....(T-615)
                                        (T-661)
The **STRENGTH** the body has will always be enough W-252
                                        W-260
Ego enjoys **STUDYING** itself T-274
                                        T-295
SUBSTITUTION T-347f
                                        T-372f
SUCCESS...SUCCEED M-40
                                        M-42
SUFFERING T-307; W-351; M-16
                              T-330; W-361; M-17
SUFFICIENT number T-30
                                        T-34
(**SUICIDE**) ....(T-96f,217,366)
                                (T-104f,233,392)
(**SUMMATION** of ACIM) ....(T-514,619; M-50)
                              (T-553,666; M-52)
SURPRISE M-59
                                        M-62
SUSPICIOUSNESS to viciousness T-79,164f,243,324
                            T-86,176f,260,348
SYMBOLS of hate...of love T-314
                                        T-337
Love's **SYMBOLS** T-539
                                        T-581
SYMBOLS of **SYMBOLS** W-214; M-51
                                W-218; M-53
("**SYMPHONIC**" arrangement of ACIM) ....(T-13)
                                      (T-16)
SYMPTOM (substitution) ....T-43,(517)
                                    T-48,(557)

Second Edition numbers in *italics*

ADDITIONS / NOTES

T

ADDITIONS / NOTES

THOUSANDS of years T-6
                                T-8
Spread joy to **THOUSANDS** on thousands T-358
                                T-383
TIME is an illusion W-252
                                W-259
(Birth of) **TIME** (and bodies)..T-408
                                T-438
Saving **TIME** (...collapse...waste/be wasted) T-6,10,363,574f
                              T-8,12,389,618f
There is no **TIME** T-544
                                T-587
TIME...world of illusion...goes backward W-291; M-4
                              W-298; M-5
    ...is set already...a trick...a sleight of hand T-511f; W-316
                              T-550f; W-324
    ...is meaningless...not exist T-5,544
                              T-7,587
    ...is neutral T-519
                              T-559
    ...is a learning device T-81f
                              T-88f
    ...is a trick W-291
                              W-298
TIME ...horizontal to vertical...thousands of years T-6
                              T-8
TIME and space...under my control T-29
                              T-33
TIME you made T-440
                              T-473
TIME (vs Space) concept...(neutrality of)...(nearer/farther) T-519f
                              T-558f
TIME of terror took the place of love T-512f
                              T-551f
TIMELESSNESS ...take the place of time T-573
                              T-617
TINY mad desire T-483
                              T-520
TINY mad idea of corruption T-389
                              T-418
TINY mad idea...remembered not to laugh T-544
                              T-586
When you feel **TIRED**....sense of strain T-42f,201
                              T-47,216
TOYS of battle T-589f; W-333,409
                              T-633; W-341,419

Second Edition numbers in *italics*

ADDITIONS / NOTES

Slowly-evolving **TRAINING** program M-25
                                                    M-26
A good **TRANSLATOR** T-106
                                                    T-115
TRAVEL but in dreams T-240
                                                    T-257
TRIALS...presented once again T-620
                                                    T-666
Not all the **TRICKS** and games you offer T-226
                                                    T-243
Last **TRUMPET** T-529
                                                    T-569
TRUST not your good intentions T-355
                                                    T-380
TRUTH is God's creation W-242
                                                    W-248
TRUTH...experienced...not be described ....(P-4); T-139; W-242
                                          (x) ; *T-150; W-248*
TRUTH returns T-613
                                                    T-660
The laws of **TRUTH** T-515
                                                    T-554

U

Spirit...is **UNAWARE** of the ego T-53
                                                    T-58
...is not **UNDERSTOOD,** but can be taught T-483
                                                    T-520
Your **UNDERSTANDING** T-353f
                                                    T-379f
The **UNDOING** process T-83; W-34,118,356,365
                                            T-90; W-34,119,366,375
Strange **UNEASINESS** (cp. isolation, loss and loneliness T-517)..T-436
                      (*"*   *"*   *"*   *T-556).* *T-468*
Beware the temptation...**UNFAIRLY** treated T-523
                                                    T-563
UNFORGIVING mind..W-210
                                                    W-214
UNHOLY Instant T-410
                                                    T-440
UNHOLY Relationship T-408,435
                                                  T-438,467
UNIVERSAL Course ....(P-2); M-3
                                                  (ix) ; M-3
UNIVERSAL theology...experience ....(P-2); M-73
                                                  (ix) ; M-77

Second Edition numbers in *italics*

ADDITIONS / NOTES

("UNPARDONABLE") sin ....(T-456)
(T-491)
UNSEALED and open mind T-613
T-660
Your **UNWILLINGNESS** T-323
T-347
UPSIDE-down thinking in the New Testament ....T-87,(375,515)
T-95,(403,554)

V

VAGUE unanswered question ....T-457,(613)
T-491,(659)
VALUE (unwillingness/willingness to question) T-239,464
T-256,499
VEIL of ignorance T-615
T-661
Suspiciousness to **VICIOUSNESS** T-79,164f,243
T-86,176f,260
He is the **VICTIM** T-539
T-581
(**VIDEO** tape) concept..(T-348; M-4)
(T-373; M-5)
Be **VIGILANT** T-100f
T-108f
VISION (spiritual) T-18f,410-14
T-22,440-44
VISION of Christ ....(P-6); T-492,618; W-47
(xiii); T-529,665; W-47
No other **VOICE** M-33
M-34

W

The **"WAGES"** of sin T-375
T-402
WAR is impossible T-452f
T-486f
The **WAY** to certainty T-363,425,512,563f; W-105f,284
T-389,456,551,607f ; W-106f,291
Gentle **WAY** of kindness T-568
T-611
Along the **WAY** of truth T-468
T-504
"WAY" is means for HS T-548
T-590

Second Edition numbers in *italics*

ADDITIONS / NOTES

WEARYING yourself T-43
T-47
God WEEPS T-82
T-89
WHAT is it for? (Ask) T-16,341,479
T-19,366,515
WHEN to come to him in silence W-477
W-487
WHOLENESS (vs lack) T-4
T-6
The WILL of God T-130,516; W-175
T-140,556; W-178
WILLINGNESS (little) T-354
T-380
WILLINGNESS (perfect) T-205,323
T-220,347
WILLINGNESS (simple) T-323
T-347
WIPE away (all tears) (Rev.21:4) T-526; W-445
T-566; W-455
WISDOM...is innocence T-33f; M-27,68
T-38f; M-28,71
WISH ... WISHES T-44,131,353,516,613
T-49,142,379,555,659
WITNESSES (to sin, ego; to love, Holy Spirit) T-214f,537
T-230f,579
WITNESSES are messengers T-215
T-231
WORLD, What is? T-576; W-237,403
T-620; W-243,413
  (made as an attack on God) W-403
  W-413
  (causeless) T-551
  T-594
  (delusional system) T-220
  T-236
  (fantasy) W-34
  W-34
  (a little gap) T-554
  T-597
  (an hallucination) T-413; W-34
  T-443; W-34
  (based on this insane belief) W-245
  W-252
  (God did not create it) W-23,85,403,476; M-81
  W-23,87,403,512; M-85

Page 35

ADDITIONS / NOTES

(end in laughter) M-36
                                  M-37

(the making of) T-348
                                  T-373

(not "outside") T-206
                                  T-222

(opposite of Heaven) T-317
                                  T-341

(over long ago) T-547
                                  T-589

(real purpose) T-11
                                  T-14

(Real) T-352
                                  T-378

(its sense of threat) W-245
                                  W-252

(a symbol of death) T-207
                                  T-222

(unhappy) T-89
                                  T-97

(so vast...incredible...the making of) T-347f
                                  T-372f

WORLDS (outer) T-239
                                  T-257

       (three) T-349
                                  T-375

Your **WORTH** T-49
                                  T-54

WRATH of God ....T-(424),498; (W-278)
                            T-(454),535; (W-285)

Y

As **YOU** are God T-312
                                  T-336

YOU are not at home T-208
                                  T-224

YOU do not know (what you need) T-239
                                  T-256

YOU have heard T-310
                                  T-333

Second Edition numbers in *italics*

ADDITIONS / NOTES

SECTION II:
TEXT CHAPTER/SECTION HEADINGS
ALPHABETICAL

Page   *Page*

A

Above the Battleground..T-461 *T-496*
THE **ACCEPTANCE** OF THE ATONEMENT - CH.9..T-149 *T-160*
The **Acceptance** of Reality..T-149 *T-160*
The **Acceptance** of Your Brother....................................T-161 *T-173*
The **Agreement** to Join...T-553 *T-596*
The **Altar** of God..T-17 *T-21*
The **Alternate** to Dreams of Fear....................................T-557 *T-600*
The **Alternate** to Projection..T-88 *T-96*
The **Answer** to Prayer..T-152 *T-163*
The **Anti-Christ**..T-575 *T-619*
The **Appointed** Friend..T-513 *T-553*
The **Ark** of Safety...T-561 *T-604*
At Home in God...T-168 *T-182*
The **Atonement** as Defense...T-15 *T-19*
Atonement and Miracles...T-6 *T-8*
Atonement Without Sacrifice..T-32 *T-36*
THE **ATTAINMENT** OF PEACE - CHAP.19.................T-371 *T-398*
Attainment of the Real World...T-236 *T-254*
The **Attraction** of Love for Love.....................................T-217 *T-233*
THE **AWAKENING** - CHAP.29.......................................T-563 *T-606*

B

The **Basis** of the Dream..T-350 *T-375*
Beyond All Idols...T-586 *T-630*
Beyond All Symbols..T-531 *T-572*
Beyond the Body...T-358 *T-384*
Beyond Perception..T-39 *T-44*
The **Body** as a Means of Communication.......................T-140 *T-151*
The **Body** as Means or End...T-143 *T-155*
The **Borderland**...T-508 *T-546*
The **Branching** of the Road..T-444 *T-477*
The **Bridge** to the Real World...T-321 *T-345*
Bringing Fantasy to Truth..T-327 *T-351*

Second Edition numbers in *italics*

ADDITIONS / NOTES

C

The **Call** for Faith...T-342 *T-367*
Cause and Effect..T-27 *T-31*
The **Changeless** Dwelling Place.............................T-570 *T-614*
Changeless Reality...T-597 *T-642*
The **Choice** for Completion....................................T-317 *T-341*
Choose Once Again..T-619 *T-666*
The **Christ** in You...T-473 *T-509*
Christmas as the End of Sacrifice.........................T-304 *T-327*
The **Circle** of Atonement..T-262 *T-282*
The **Closing** of the Gap...T-563 *T-606*
The **Cloud** of Guilt..T-242 *T-260*
The **Coming** of the Guest..T-565 *T-608*
The **Condition** of Reality...T-194 *T-210*
The **Conditions** of Learning....................................T-251 *T-270*
The **Conditions** of Peace...T-345 *T-370*
The **Confusion** of Pain and Joy..............................T-124 *T-133*
The **Consistency** of Means and End........................T-409 *T-439*
The **Correction** of Error..T-155 *T-166*
Creating versus the Self-Image..............................T-44 *T-49*
Creation and Communication..................................T-63 *T-69*

D

The **Decision** to Forget..T-169 *T-183*
The **Decision** for God..T-81 *T-88*
The **Decision** for Guiltlessness...............................T-255 *T-274*
The **Denial** of God...T-175 *T-189*
The **Difference** Between Imprisonment and Freedom......T-129 *T-139*
The **Direction** of the Curriculum............................T-128 *T-138*
Distortions of Miracle Impulses.............................T-12 *T-15*
Dream Roles...T-568 *T-612*
The **Dreamer** of the Dream.....................................T-539 *T-581*
The **"Dynamics"** of the Ego....................................T-188 *T-202*

E

The **Ego**-Body Illusion...T-59 *T-65*
The **Ego** and False Autonomy..................................T-51 *T-56*
The **Ego's** Use of Guilt..T-77 *T-83*
The **End** of Doubt..T-283 *T-304*
The **End** of Illusions..T-323 *T-347*
The **End** of Injustice..T-522 *T-562*
The **End** of Sickness..T-173 *T-187*
Entering the Ark...T-402 *T-432*

Second Edition numbers in *italics*

ADDITIONS / NOTES

The **Equality** of Miracles.................................T-272　*T-293*
Error and the Ego...T-37　*T-41*
The **Escape** from Darkness...............................T-8　*T-11*
The **Extension** of the Kingdom........................T-122　*T-132*

F

Faith, Belief and Vision...................................T-421　*T-451*
Fear and Conflict..T-24　*T-28*
The **Fear** to Look Within.................................T-423　*T-454*
The **Fear** of Healing..T-528　*T-568*
The **Fear** of Redemption..................................T-225　*T-242*
THE **FINAL** VISION - CHAP.31.....................T-600　*T-645*
Finding the Present..T-233　*T-250*
For They Have Come......................................T-521　*T-560*
The **Forgiven** World.......................................T-328　*T-352*
Forgiveness and the End of Time.....................T-572　*T-615*
FORGIVENESS & THE HOLY RELATIONSHIP-CH.17..T-327　*351*
THE **FORGIVENESS** OF ILLUSIONS - CHAP.16........T-307　*T-330*
The **Forgiveness** of Specialness.......................T-470　*T-505*
The **Forgiving** Dream.....................................T-577　*T-622*
The **Forgotten** Song..T-415　*T-445*
Freedom of Will..T-585　*T-629*
From Darkness to Light...................................T-184　*T-198*
From Perception to Knowledge........................T-240　*T-258*
From Vigilance to Peace..................................T-114　*T-123*
The **Function** of the Miracle Worker.................T-21　*T-24*
The **Function** of Reason..................................T-425　*T-456*
The **Function** of Time.....................................T-228　*T-245*

G

The **Gift** of Freedom.......................................T-133　*T-143*
The **Gift** of Lilies...T-397　*T-426*
The **Gifts** of Fatherhood.................................T-180　*T-194*
THE **GIFTS** OF THE KINGDOM - CHAP.7...........T-104　*T-112*
THE **GOAL** OF SPECIALNESS - CHAP.24..........T-464　*T-499*
GOD OR THE EGO - CHAP.11..........................T-179　*T-193*
The **God** of Sickness.......................................T-171　*T-184*
God's Witnesses..T-567　*T-611*
Grandeur versus **Grandiosity** ....T-165　*T-177*
The **Greater** Joining.......................................T-555　*T-598*
The **Guide** to Salvation...................................T-72　*T-78*
The **Guiltless** Son of God...............................T-223　*T-239*
THE **GUILTLESS** WORLD - CHAP.13...............T-220　*T-236*
Guiltlessness and Invulnerability.....................T-221　*T-237*

Second Edition numbers in *italics*

ADDITIONS / NOTES

H

The **Happy** Dream...T-357 _T-382_
The **Happy** Learner..T-252 _T-272_
The **Healed** Relationship......................................T-337 _T-362_
Healing and the Changeless of Mind..................T-111 _T-119_
THE **HEALING** OF THE DREAM - CHAP.27.............T-525 _T-565_
Healing and Faith..T-371 _T-398_
HEALING AND WHOLENESS - CHAP.5...................T-66 _T-72_
Healing as Corrected Perception.........................T-146 _T-157_
Healing as the Recognition of Truth....................T-109 _T-117_
Healing as Release from Fear...............................T-19 _T-23_
Heralds of Eternity..T-404 _T-434_
The **"Hero"** of the Dream.....................................T-543 _T-585_
The **Holy** Encounter...T-131 _T-141_
THE **HOLY** INSTANT - CHAP.15............................T-280 _T-301_
The **Holy** Instant and the Attraction of God.........T-299 _T-322_
The **Holy** Instant and the Laws of God.................T-292 _T-314_
The **Holy** Instant and Special Relationships..........T-290 _T-312_
The **Holy** Meeting Place.......................................T-269 _T-289_
THE **HOLY** SPIRIT'S CURRICULUM - CHAP.12........T-200 _T-215_
The **Holy** Spirit's Plan of Forgiveness..................T-156 _T-168_
Holy Week..T-396 _T-425_

I

I Need do Nothing..T-362 _T-388_
THE **IDOLS** OF SICKNESS - CHAP.10......................T-168 _T-181_
The **Inheritance** of God's Son..............................T-186 _T-200_
The **Illusion** of Needs...T-11 _T-13_
The **Illusion** and the Reality of Love....................T-313 _T-337_
THE **ILLUSIONS** OF THE EGO - CHAP.4...................T-47 _T-52_
The **Immediacy** of Salvation................................T-519 _T-558_
The **Inner** Shift...T-433 _T-465_
THE **INNOCENT** PERCEPTION - CHAP.3...................T-32 _T-36_
The **Investment** in Reality...................................T-205 _T-220_
The **Invitation** to Healing...................................T-182 _T-197_
The **Invitation** to the Holy Spirit.........................T-66 _T-73_
The **Irreconcilable** Beliefs...................................T-452 _T-486_

J

THE **JOURNEY** BACK - CHAP.8...............................T-128 _T-138_
Judgment and the Authority Problem...................T-41 _T-46_
The **Judgment** of the Holy Spirit.........................T-200 _T-215_
THE **JUSTICE** OF GOD - CHAP.25...........................T-482 _T-518_
The **Justice** of Heaven...T-501 _T-538_
Justice Returned to Love.....................................T-497 _T-534_

Second Edition numbers in _italics_

ADDITIONS / NOTES

The **Justification** for Forgiveness...................................T-593   *T-638*

L

The **Last** Step...T-104   *T-112*
The **Last** Unanswered Question...................................T-430   *T-461*
The **Law** of the Kingdom...T-105   *T-114*
The **Laws** of Chaos...T-455   *T-489*
The **Laws** of Healing...T-514   *T-553*
The **Lessons** of the Holy Spirit.................................T-95   *T-103*
  I. "To Have, Give All to All"...............................T-96   *T-104*
  II. "To Have Peace, Teach Peace to Learn It"..................T-98   *T-106*
  III. "Be Vigilant Only for God and His Kingdom".........T-100   *T-108*
THE **LESSONS** OF **LOVE** - CHAP.6...........................T-84   *T-91*
The **Light** of Communication.....................................T-264   *T-285*
The **Light** in the Dream...T-352   *T-378*
The **Light** of the Holy Relationship.............................T-447   *T-480*
The **Light** You Bring..T-489   *T-526*
The **Link** to Truth..T-482   *T-518*
The **Little** Garden..T-364   *T-390*
The **Little** Hindrance...T-511   *T-549*
The **Little** Willingness...T-354   *T-380*
Littleness versus Magnitude....................................T-285   *T-306*
Looking Within...T-213   *T-229*
Love Without Conflict..T-54   *T-60*

M

Many Forms; One Correction.....................................T-506   *T-544*
The **Meaning** of the Last Judgment...............................T-29   *T-33*
THE **MEANING** OF MIRACLES - CHAP.1...........................T-1   *T-3*
The **Meeting** Place..T-478   *T-514*
The **Message** of the Crucifixion.................................T-84   *T-91*
The **Message** of the Holy Relationship...........................T-436   *T-468*
Miracles as True Perception....................................T-34   *T-38*

N

The **Needless** Sacrifice...T-294   *T-317*
THE **NEW** BEGINNING - CHAP.30................................T-581   *T-625*
The **New** Interpretation...T-595   *T-640*

O

The **Obstacles** to Peace...T-379   *T-406*
  I. The Desire to Get Rid of It.......................T-380   *T-407*
      The Attraction of Guilt.....................T-382   *T-410*

Second Edition numbers in *italics*

ADDITIONS / NOTES

II. The Belief the Body is Valuable
    for What It Offers..T-384   *T-412*
    The Attraction of Pain..................................T-386   *T-414*
III. The Attraction of Death................................T-388   *T-416*
    The Incorruptible Body.................................T-389   *T-417*
IV. The Fear of God..T-391   *T-420*
    The Lifting of the Veil..................................T-393   *T-421*
The **Only** Answer..T-92   *T-100*
The **Only** Purpose..T-590   *T-635*
The **Only** Real Relationship................................T-298   *T-320*
The **Origins** of Separation.................................T-14   *T-17*

P

THE **PASSING** OF THE DREAM - CHAP.18..............T-347   *T-372*
The **Peace** of Heaven..T-248   *T-266*
Perception and Choice......................................T-487   *T-523*
Perception versus Knowledge............................T-35   *T-40*
The **Picture** of Crucifixion.................................T-525   *T-565*
The **Power** of Holiness.......................................T-309   *T-332*
Practicing the Holy Instant...............................T-288   *T-309*
The **Present** Memory..T-547   *T-589*
Principles of Miracles.......................................T-1   *T-3*
The **Problem** and the Answer.............................T-195   *T-211*

Q

The **Quiet** Answer...T-533   *T-574*

R

The **Real** Alternative..T-607   *T-653*
The **Reality** of the Kingdom...............................T-107   *T-116*
Reason and the Forms of Error...........................T-442   *T-474*
Reason versus Madness......................................T-428   *T-459*
REASON AND PERCEPTION - CHAP.21..................T-415   *T-445*
Recognizing the Spirit......................................T-614   *T-660*
The **Reflection** of Holiness................................T-270   *T-291*
Release from Guilt...T-244   *T-262*
The **Relinquishment** of Attack............................T-91   *T-99*
The **Responsibility** for Sight.............................T-417   *T-448*
Revelation, Time and Miracles...........................T-4   *T-7*
Reversing Effect and Cause...............................T-550   *T-592*
The **Reward** of Teaching.....................................T-311   *T-334*
The **Rewards** of God...T-61   *T-67*
Right Teaching and Right Learning.....................T-47   *T-53*
The **Rock** of Salvation..T-494   *T-531*
Rules for Decision..T-581   *T-625*

Second Edition numbers in *italics*

ADDITIONS / NOTES

S

The **"Sacrifice"** of Oneness...T-504 *T-542*
Salvation from Fear...T-475 *T-511*
SALVATION & THE HOLY RELATIONSHIP-CH.22 T-435 *T-467*
Salvation Without Compromise...T-460 *T-495*
The **Sane** Curriculum...T-209 *T-225*
The **Savior** from the Dark...T-484 *T-520*
The **Savior's** Vision...T-615 *T-662*
The **Secret** Vows...T-559 *T-602*
Seek Not Outside Yourself...T-573 *T-617*
Seeking and Finding...T-207 *T-223*
The **Self-Accused** T-606 *T-651*
Self Concept versus **Self** T-610 *T-656*
THE **SEPARATION** AND THE ATONEMENT - CH.2...T-14 *T-17*
Setting the Goal...T-340 *T-365*
Shadows of the Past...T-330 *T-354*
Sharing Perception with the Holy Spirit...T-266 *T-287*
The **Simplicity** of Salvation...T-600 *T-645*
Sin as an Adjustment...T-399 *T-429*
Sin versus Error...T-374 *T-402*
The **Special** Function...T-492 *T-529*
Special Principles of Miracle Workers...T-23 *T-27*
Specialness versus Sinlessness...T-472 *T-507*
Specialness as a Substitute for Love...T-464 *T-499*
The **State** of Grace...T-126 *T-136*
The **State** of Sinlessness...T-490 *T-527*
The **Substitute** Reality...T-347 *T-372*

T

Teaching and Healing...T-74 *T-81*
TEACHING FOR TRUTH - CHAP.14...T-251 *T-270*
The **Temple** of the Holy Spirit...T-406 *T-436*
The **Test** of Truth...T-275 *T-296*
This Need Not Be...T-57 *T-62*
Time and Eternity...T-79 *T-86*
The **Time** of Rebirth...T-301 *T-324*
The **Totality** of the Kingdom...T-117 *T-127*
THE **TRANSITION** - CHAP.26...T-504 *T-542*
The **Treachery** of Specialness...T-466 *T-502*
The **Treasure** of God...T-137 *T-148*
True Empathy...T-307 *T-330*
The **Truth** Behind Illusions...T-588 *T-633*
The **Two** Emotions...T-230 *T-247*
The **Two** Evaluations...T-163 *T-175*
The **Two** Pictures...T-333 *T-357*

Second Editions numbers in *italics*

ADDITIONS / NOTES

The **Two** Uses of Time..T-280 *T-301*
The **Two** Worlds...T-367 *T-393*

U

The **Unbelievable** Belief...T-120 *T-129*
The **Undivided** Will of the Sonship...................................T-136 *T-146*
THE **UNDOING** OF FEAR - CHAP.28............................T-547 *T-589*
The **Unhealed** Healer..T-159 *T-171*
The **Unreality** of Sin...T-376 *T-404*

V

The **Vision** of Christ...T-211 *T-227*
THE **VISION** OF HOLINESS - CHAP.20........................T-396 *T-425*
The **Vision** of Sinlessness..T-411 *T-441*
The **Voice** for God...T-69 *T-75*

W

Waking to Redemption..T-192 *T-207*
Walking with Christ...T-603 *T-648*
THE **WAR** AGAINST YOURSELF - CHAP.23...............T-451 *T-485*
The **Way** to Remember God...T-203 *T-218*
Weakness and Defensiveness..T-445 *T-478*
Where Sin Has Left..T-509 *T-548*
Wholeness and Spirit..T-9 *T-12*
The **Witnesses** to Sin...T-537 *T-579*

Y

Your Brother's Sinlessness...T-438 *T-471*
Your Function in the Atonement...T-259 *T-279*

ADDITIONS / NOTES

WORKBOOK CHAPTER HEADINGS
ALPHABETICAL

	Lsn.	Pg.	*Pg.*

A

"**ABOVE ALL** else I want to see."	27	42	*42*
"**ABOVE ALL** else I want to see things differently."	28	43	*43*
"**A** happy outcome to all things is sure."	292	434	*444*
"**A** meaningless world engenders fear."	13	21	*21*
"**ALL** fear is past and only **LOVE** is here."	293	435	*445*
"**ALL** gifts I give my brothers are my own."	316	448	*458*
"**ALL** gifts my brothers give belong to me."	315	448	*458*
"**ALL** that I give is given to myself."	126	222	*227*
"**ALL** things are echoes of the Voice for God."	151	271	*278*
"**ALL** things are lessons God....... learn."	193	357	*367*
"**ALL** things I think I see reflect ideas."	325	454	*464*
"**AND** God Himself shall wipe away all tears."	301	440	*450*
"**ANGER** must come from judgment. Judgment is The weapon I would use against myself, To keep the miracle away from me."	347	467	*477*

B

"**BE** in my mind, my Father, through the day."	232	398	*408*
"**BEYOND** this world there is a world I want."	129	229	*235*
"**BY** grace I live. By grace I am released."	169	315	*323*

C

"**CONFLICTING** wishes cannot be my will."	307	443	*453*
"**CREATION'S** freedom promises my own."	279	426	*436*
"**CREATION'S** gentleness is all I see."	265	418	*428*
"**CHRIST'S** is the vision I will use today."	271	422	*432*

E

"**ETERNAL** holiness abides in me."	299	438	*448*
EPILOGUE		477	487

F

"**FATHER**, I will but to remember You."	231	398	*408*
"**FATHER**, my freedom is in You alone."	321	452	*462*
"**FATHER**, today I am Your Son again."	234	399	*409*
"**FEAR** binds the world. **FORGIVENESS** sets it free."	332	458	*468*
"**FEAR** is not justified in any form."	240	402	*412*

Second Edition numbers in *italics*

ADDITIONS / NOTES

What is **FORGIVENESS**?...#*1*. 391 *401*
"**FORGIVENESS** ends all suffering and loss.".............249 408 *418*
"**FORGIVENESS** ends the dream of conflict here.".......333 459 *469*
"**FORGIVENESS** is my function as the light of
  the world."..62 100 *104*
"**FORGIVENESS** is the key to happiness."....................121 210 *214*
"**FORGIVENESS** is the only gift I give.".......................297 437 *447*
"**FORGIVENESS** lets me know that minds are joined."....336 460 *470*
"**FORGIVENESS** offers everything I want.".................122 213 *217*
"I let **FORGIVENESS** rest upon all things,
For thus **FORGIVENESS** will be given me."..................342 464 *474*
"Today I claim the gifts **FORGIVENESS** gives.".........334 459 *469*
"Without **FORGIVENESS** I will still be blind."............247 407 *417*

G

"**GIVE** me your blessing, holy Son of God.".................161 297 *304*
"**GOD**, being **LOVE**, is also happiness.".................103 182 *185*
"**GOD** did not create a meaningless world."..................14 23 *23*
"**GOD** goes with me wherever I go."...........................41 63 *63*
"**GOD** has condemned me not. No more do I."...............228 395 *405*
"**GOD** in His mercy wills that I be saved."...................235 400 *410*
"**GOD IS** in everything I see."...................................29 45 *45*
"**GOD IS** in everything I see because...mind."..............30 47 *47*
"**GOD IS** my Father, and He loves His Son."...............224 393 *403*
"**GOD IS** my Father, and His Son loves Him.".............225 394 *404*
"**GOD IS** my life. I have no life but His.".....................223 393 *403*
"**GOD IS** my refuge and security.".............................261 416 *426*
"**GOD IS** my Source. I cannot see apart
from Him."..43 67 *67*
"**GOD IS** my Strength. Vision is His gift.".................42 65 *65*
"**GOD IS** the Light in which I see.".............................44 69 *69*
"**GOD IS** the **LOVE** in which I forgive.".................46 73 *73*
"**GOD IS** the Mind with which I think.".......................45 71 *71*
"**GOD IS** the only goal I have today."..........................256 412 *412*
"**GOD IS** the Strength in which I trust."......................47 75 *75*
"**GOD IS** with me. I live and move in Him."................222 392 *402*
"**GOD'S** answer is some form of peace. All pain
Is healed; all misery replaced with joy.
All prison doors are opened. And all sin
Is understood as merely a mistake.".............................359 474 *484*
"**GOD'S** healing Voice protects all things today.".........275 424 *434*
"**GOD'S** peace and joy are mine."..............................105 185 *188*
"**GOD'S** Voice speaks to me all through the day.".........49 78 *78*
"**GOD'S** Will for me is perfect happiness."..................101 179 *182*

Second Edition numbers in *italics*

ADDITIONS / NOTES

H

"HEAVEN is the decision I must make.".......................138   257 *264*
"HOLDING grievances is an attack on God's
  plan for salvation."...72   122 *124*
"HOW can illusions satisfy God's Son?".......................272   422 *432*

I

What am I?...#*14*.   469 *479*
"I AM affected only by my thoughts.".......................338   461 *471*
"I AM among the ministers of God.".............................154   281 *288*
"I AM as God created me."...94   162 *164*
"I AM as God created me."...110   195 *199*
"I AM as God created me."...162   300 *307*
"I AM at home. Fear is the stranger here.".................160   295 *302*
"I AM blessed as a Son of God.".................................40   62 *62*
"I AM determined to see."..20   31 *31*
"I AM determined to see things differently.".................21   32 *32*
"I AM entitled to miracles."..77   135 *137*
"I AM entrusted with the gifts of God.".......................166   308 *315*
"I AM forever an effect of God.".................................326   454 *464*
"I AM in danger nowhere in the world.".......................244   405 *415*
"I AM in need of nothing but the truth.".......................251   410 *420*
"I AM never upset for the reason I think.".....................5   8   *8*
"I AM not a body. I am free."......................................199   372 *382*
"I AM not alone in experiencing the effects
  of my seeing."..18   29 *29*
"I AM not alone in experiencing the effects
  of my thoughts."...19   30 *30*
"I AM not asked to make a sacrifice
  To find the mercy and the peace of God.".................343   465 *475*
"I AM not the victim of the world I see."......................31   48 *48*
"I AM one Self, united with my Creator."......................95   164 *166*
"I AM spirit."...97   170 *172*
"I AM surrounded by the LOVE of God.".....................264   417 *427*
"I AM sustained by the LOVE of God.".........................50   79 *79*
"I AM the holy Son of God Himself.".............................191   353 *363*
"I AM the light of the world.".......................................61   101 *102*
"I AM under no laws but God's."...................................76   132 *134*
"I AM upset because I see a meaningless world."...........12   19 *19*
"I AM upset because I see something that is not there."....6   10 *10*
"I bless the world because I bless myself.".....................187   345 *354*
"I call upon God's Name and on my own."......................183   334 *342*
"I came for the salvation of the world."........................319   450 *460*
"I can attack but my own sinlessness,
  And it is only that which keeps me safe.".................341   464 *474*
"I can be free of suffering today."...............................340   462 *472*

ADDITIONS / NOTES

"I can be hurt by nothing but my thoughts."..................281   428 *438*

"I can elect to change all thoughts that hurt."................284   429 *439*

"I can escape from the world I see by giving
up attack thoughts."..23   34 *34*

"I can give up but what was never real."......................322   452 *462*

"I choose to see my brother's sinlessness"..................335   460 *470*

"I choose the joy of God instead of pain."....................190   351 *361*

"I choose the second place to gain the first."...............328   455 *465*

"I could see peace instead of this."................................34   51 *51*

"I do not know what anything is for."............................25   38 *38*

"I do not perceive my own best interests."....................24   36 *36*

"I do not understand anything I see."..............................3   5 *5*

"I feel the LOVE of God within me now."....................189   349 *359*

"I follow in the way appointed me."..............................317   449 *459*

"I give my life to God to guide today."..........................233   399 *409*

"I give the miracles I have received."............................159   293 *300*

"I gladly make the 'sacrifice' of fear."...........................323   453 *463*

"I have a function God would have me fill."..................192   355 *365*

"I have already chosen what You will."..........................329   456 *466*

"I have given everything I see...all the
meaning that it has for me."..2   4 *4*

"I have invented the world I see."....................................32   49 *49*

"I have no cause for anger or for fear,
For You surround me. And in every need
That I perceive, Your grace suffices me."....................348   467 *477*

"I have no neutral thoughts."..16   26 *26*

"I judge all things as I would have them be."...............311   446 *456*

"I let FORGIVENESS rest upon all things,
For thus FORGIVENESS will be given me."................342   464 *474*

"I loose the world from all I thought it was."...............132   236 *242*

"I love You, Father, and I love Your Son."...................298   437 *447*

"I merely follow, for I would not lead."........................324   453 *463*

"I need but call and You will answer me."....................327   455 *465*

"I offer only miracles today,
For I would have them be returned to me."..................345   466 *476*

"I place the future in the Hands of God."......................194   360 *370*

"I rest in God."..109   193 *197*

"I rule my mind, which I alone must rule."....................236   400 *410*

"I see all things as I would have them be."...................312   446 *456*

"I see no neutral things."..17   28 *28*

"I see nothing as it is now."...9   15 *15*

"I see only the past."...7   11 *11*

"I seek a future different from the past."......................314   447 *457*

"I seek but what belongs to me in truth."....................104   183 *186*

"I share God's Will for happiness for me."...................102   181 *184*

"I thank my Father for His gifts to me."......................123   216 *220*

"I trust my brothers, who are one with me."................181   329 *337*

"I walk with God in perfect holiness."..........................156   287 *294*

Second Edition numbers in *italics*

ADDITIONS / NOTES

"**I want** the peace of God."...185 339 *348*
"**I will accept** atonement for myself.".......................139 260 *267*
"**I will accept** my part in God's plan for
  salvation."...98 172 *174*
"**I will be still** an instant and go home.".................182 331 *339*
"**I will not be afraid** of **LOVE** today.".................282 428 *438*
"**I will not fear** to look within today.".....................309 444 *454*
"**I will not hurt** myself again today.".......................330 456 *466*
"**I will not use** the body's eyes today.".....................270 420 *430*
"**I will not value** what is valueless.".........................133 239 *245*
"**I will receive** whatever I request.".........................339 462 *472*
"**I will step back** and **LET** him lead the way.".......155 284 *291*
"**I will** there be light."...73 125 *127*
"**IF** I am bound, my Father is not free.".....................278 425 *435*
"**IF** I defend myself I am attacked.".........................135 245 *252*
"**IN** fearlessness and **LOVE** I spend today.".........310 444 *454*
"**IN** me salvation's means and end are one.".............318 449 *459*
"**IN** my defenselessness my safety lies.".................153 277 *284*
"**IN** quiet I receive God's Word today.".................125 220 *225*
"**INTO** his presence would I enter now.".................157 289 *296*
INTRODUCTION...(PART I)..................................   1   *1*
INTRODUCTION 328 *336*
INTRODUCTION...(PART II)................................ 388 *398*
INTRODUCTION...(Final Lessons)....................... 475 *485*
"**IT** can be but my gratitude I earn.".........................197 367 *377*
"**IT** can be but myself I crucify.".............................196 364 *374*
"**IT** is impossible to see two worlds.".......................130 231 *237*

J

"**JUDGMENT** and **LOVE** are opposites. From one
Come all the sorrows of the world. But from
The other comes the peace of God Himself.".................352 470 *480*

L

"**LET** all things be exactly as they are.".....................268 419 *429*
"**LET** every voice but God's be still in me.".............254 411 *421*
"**LET** me be still and listen to the truth.".................106 187 *190*
"**LET** me forget my brother's past today.".................288 431 *441*
"**LET** me not bind Your Son with laws I made.".........277 425 *435*
"**LET** me not forget my function.".............................64 105 *106*
"**LET** me not see myself as limited.".........................250 408 *418*
"**LET** me perceive **FORGIVENESS** as it is.".........134 242 *248*
"**LET** me perceive no differences today.".................262 416 *426*
"**LET** me recognize my problems have been solved.".....80 141 *143*
"**LET** me recognize the problem so it can be solved.".....79 139 *141*

Second Edition numbers in *italics*

ADDITIONS / NOTES

"**LET** me remember God created me."..............260 414 *424*
"**LET** me remember I am one with God."..............124 218 *222*
"**LET** me remember that my goal is God."..............258 413 *423*
"**LET** me remember that there is no sin."..............259 414 *424*
"**LET** me remember what my purpose is."..............257 413 *423*
"**LET** miracles replace all grievances."..............78 137 *139*
"**LET** not my mind deny the Thought of God."..............165 306 *313*
"**LET** not my world obscure the sight of Christ."..............304 441 *451*
"**LIGHT** and joy and peace abide in me."..............93 159 *161*
"All fear is past and only **LOVE** is here."..............293 435 *445*
"God, being **LOVE,** is also happiness."..............103 182 *185*
"God is the **LOVE** in which I forgive."..............46 73 *73*
"I am surrounded by the **LOVE** of God."..............264 417 *427*
"I am sustained by the **LOVE** of God."..............50 79 *79*
"I feel the **LOVE** of God within me now."..............189 349 *359*
"I will not be afraid of **LOVE** today."..............282 428 *438*
"**LOVE** created me like Itself."..............67 112 *113*
"**LOVE** holds no grievances."..............68 114 *115*
"**LOVE** is the way I walk in gratitude."..............195 362 *372*
"**LOVE,** Which created me, is what I am."..............229 396 *406*
"There is no **LOVE** but God's."..............127 225 *230*

M

"**MIRACLES** mirror God's eternal Love.
To offer them is to remember Him,
And through His memory to save the world."..............350 468 *478*
"**MIRACLES** are seen in light."..............91 154 *156*
"**MIRACLES** are seen in light, and light and
 strength are one."..............92 157 *159*
"**MY attack thoughts** are attacking my
 invulnerability."..............26 40 *40*
"**MY body** is a wholly neutral thing."..............294 435 *445*
"**MY eyes,** my tongue, my hands, my feet today
Have but one purpose; to be given Christ
To use to bless the world with miracles."..............353 471 *481*
"**MY Father** gives all power unto me."..............320 450 *460*
"**MY grievances** hide the light of the world
 in me."..............69 116 *117*
"**MY happiness** and my function are one."..............66 109 *110*
"**MY heart** is beating in the peace of God."..............267 419 *429*
"**MY holiness** blesses the world."..............37 56 *56*
"**MY holiness** envelops everything I see."..............36 55 *55*
"**MY holiness** is my salvation."..............39 60 *60*
"**MY holiness** shines bright and clear today."..............285 430 *440*
"**MY holy Self** abides in you, God's Son."..............266 418 *428*
"**MY holy vision** sees all things as pure."..............263 417 *427*
"**MY home** awaits me. I will hasten there."..............226 394 *404*

ADDITIONS / NOTES

"MY meaningless thoughts...meaningless world."..........11   18   *18*
"MY mind is part of God's. I am very holy."................35   53   *53*
"MY mind is preoccupied with past thoughts."..............8   13   *13*
"MY only function is the one God gave me."...................65   107   *108*
"MY part is essential to God's plan for
  salvation."..100   177   *180*
"MY present happiness is all I see.".............................290   432   *442*
"MY salvation comes from me."...................................70   118   *119*
"MY Self is ruler of the universe.".................................253   411   *421*
"MY sight goes forth to look upon Christ's face.".........269   420   *430*
"MY sinless brother is my guide to peace.
My sinful brother is my guide to pain.
And which I choose to see I will behold.".....................351   470   *480*
"MY sinlessness protects me from all harm.".................337   461   *471*
"MY thoughts are images that I have made."..................15   25   *25*
"MY thoughts do not mean anything.".............................10   16   *16*
"MY true identity abides in You.".................................283   429   *439*

N

"NO call to God can be unheard nor left
Unanswered. And of this I can be sure;
His answer is the one I really want.".............................358   473   *483*
"NO one can fail who seeks to reach the truth.".............131   233   *239*
"NOTHING I see...means anything.".................................1   3   *3*
"NOW are we one with Him Who is our Source.".........164   304   *311*
"NOW let a new perception come to me."....................313   447   *457*
"NOW will I seek and find the peace of God.".............230   396   *406*
"NOW would I be as God created me."........................237   401   *411*

O

"ON my decision all salvation rests."............................238   401   *411*
"ONLY an instant does this world endure."..................300   438   *448*
"ONLY God's plan for salvation will work."..................71   120   *121*
"ONLY my condemnation injures me."..........................198   369   *379*
"ONLY salvation can be said to cure."..........................140   263   *270*

P

"PEACE to my mind. Let all my thoughts be still.".......221   392   *402*
"PEACE be to me, the holy Son of God.
Peace to my brother, who is one with me.
Let all the world be blessed with peace through us.".......360   474   *484*

R

REVIEW I..Intro-60: 80-100   *80 -100*

Second Edition numbers in *italics*

ADDITIONS / NOTES

REVIEW II..Intro-90: 143-153   *145-155*
REVIEW III...Intro-120: 197-209   *201-213*
REVIEW IV...Intro-150: 266-270   *273-277*
REVIEW V...Intro-180: 321-327   *329-335*
REVIEW VI...Intro-220: 376-387   *386-397*

S

"SALVATION is my only function here."......................99   174 *177*
"SALVATION comes from my one self."......................96   167 *169*
"SALVATION of the world depends on me.".................186   342 *351*
"SICKNESS is a defense against the truth.".....................136   250 *257*
"SICKNESS is but another name for sin.
Healing is but another name for God.
The miracle is thus a call to Him."............................356   472 *482*

T

"THE gift of Christ is all I seek today.".........................306   442 *452*
"THE glory of my Father is my own.".........................239   402 *412*
"THE HOLY CHRIST is born in me today.".................303   441 *451*
"THE HOLY SPIRIT looks through me today.".............295   436 *446*
"THE HOLY SPIRIT speaks through me today.".........296   436 *446*
"THE Hush of Heaven holds my heart today.".............286   430 *440*
"THE Light has come."..75   130 *132*
"THE Light of the world brings peace to every
   mind through my FORGIVENESS."..........................63   104 *105*
"THE Name of God is my inheritance.".....................184   336 *345*
"THE past is over. It can touch me not."......................289   432 *442*
"THE peace of God is shining in me now."..................188   347 *357*
"THE power of decision is my own."...........................152   274 *281*
"THE Son of God is my Identity."...............................252   410 *420*
"THE stillness of the peace of God is mine."...............273   423 *433*
"THE Word of God is given me to speak."..................276   424 *434*
"THE world I see holds nothing that I want."...............128   227 *233*
"THERE IS a peace that Christ bestows on us.".............305   442 *452*
"THERE IS another way of looking at the world.".........33   50   *50*
"THERE IS no conflict, for my will is Yours.".............331   458 *468*
"THERE IS no cruelty in God and none in me.".............170   318 *326*
"THERE IS no death. The Son of God is free.".............163   302 *309*
"THERE IS no end to all the peace and joy,
And all the miracles that I will give,
When I accept God's Word. Why not today?".................355   472 *482*
"THERE IS no LOVE but God's."...............................127   225 *230*
"THERE IS no peace except the peace of God.".............200   374 *384*
"THERE IS no Will but God's."......................................74   128 *130*
"THERE IS nothing my holiness cannot do.".................38   58   *58*
"THERE IS nothing to fear."...48   77   *77*

Page 52

ADDITIONS / NOTES

"THERE IS one life, and that I share with God.".........167 311 *318*
"THESE thoughts do not mean anything."........................ 4 6 *6*
"THIS DAY I choose to spend in perfect peace.".........255 412 *422*
"THIS DAY is God's. It is my gift to Him.".................242 404 *414*
"THIS HOLY INSTANT is salvation come.".............241 404 *414*
"THIS HOLY INSTANT would I give to You.
Be You in charge. For I would follow You,
Certain that Your direction gives me peace.".........361-365 476 *486*
"THIS instant is the only time there is.".................308 443 *453*
"THIS IS a day of stillness and of peace.".................291 434 *444*
"THIS IS my Holy Instant of release.".................227 395 *405*
"TODAY belongs to LOVE. Let me not fear.".........274 423 *433*
"TODAY I claim the gifts FORGIVENESS gives.".....334 459 *469*
"TODAY I will judge nothing that occurs.".................243 405 *415*
"TODAY I learn to give as I receive.".................158 291 *298*
"TODAY I learn the law of LOVE; that what
I give my brother is my gift to me.".........344 465 *475*
"TODAY I let Christ's vision look upon
All things for me and judge them not, but give
Each one a miracle of LOVE instead.".........349 468 *478*
"TODAY the peace of God envelops me,
And I forget all things except His LOVE.".........346 466 *476*
"TO GIVE and to receive are one in truth.".........108 191 *195*
"TO LOVE my Father is to LOVE His Son.".........246 406 *416*
"TRUTH answers every call we make to God,
Responding first with miracles, and then
Returning unto us to be itself.".........357 473 *483*
"TRUTH will correct all errors in my mind.".........107 189 *192*

W

"WE STAND together, Christ and I, in peace
And certainty of purpose. And in Him
Is His Creator, as He is with me.".........354 471 *481*
"WHAT I see is a form of vengeance.".........22 33 *33*
"WHAT limits can I lay upon God's Son?".........280 426 *436*
WHAT AM I?.........#14. 469 *479*
WHAT IS CREATION?.........#11. 451 *461*
WHAT IS the BODY?.........#5. 415 *425*
WHAT IS the CHRIST?.........#6. 421 *431*
WHAT IS the EGO?.........#12. 457 *467*
WHAT IS FORGIVENESS?.........#1. 391 *401*
WHAT IS the HOLY SPIRIT?.........#7. 427 *437*
WHAT IS the LAST JUDGMENT?.........#10. 445 *455*
WHAT IS a MIRACLE?.........#13. 463 *473*
WHAT IS the REAL WORLD?.........#8. 433 *443*
WHAT IS SALVATION?.........#2. 397 *407*
WHAT IS the SECOND COMING?.........#9. 439 *449*

Second Edition numbers in *italics*

ADDITIONS / NOTES

Y

Second Edition numbers in *italics*

ADDITIONS / NOTES

MANUAL FOR TEACHER CHAPTERS
ALPHABETICAL

	Page	*Page*
Are **CHANGES** Required..Life Situation of God's Teachers?.	25	*26*
What are the **CHARACTERISTICS** of God's Teachers?	8	*9*
Defenselessness	12	*14*
Faithfulness	14	*15*
Generosity	13	*14*
Gentleness	11	*12*
Joy	12	*13*
Open-Mindedness	14	*16*
Patience	13	*15*
Tolerance	11	*12*
Trust	8	*9*
Development of Trust	8	*10*
How is **CORRECTION** Made?	45	*47*
What is **DEATH**?	63	*66*
Can God Be **Reached DIRECTLY**?	61	*64*
Who Are **GOD'S Teachers**?	3	*3*
How is **HEALING Accomplished**?	16	*17*
The **Function** of the Teacher of God	18	*19*
The Perceived **Purpose** of Sickness	16	*17*
The **Shift** in Perception	16	*17*
Is **HEALING Certain** ?	19	*20*
How are **HEALING and ATONEMENT Related**?	53	*55*
Should **HEALING be Repeated**?	21	*22*
Does **Jesus** Have a **Special Place in HEALING**?	55	*58*
What is the Role of **Words** in **HEALING**?	51	*53*
HOW is Correction Made?	45	*47*
HOW is Healing Accomplished?	16	*17*
The **Function** of the Teacher of God	18	*19*
The Perceived **Purpose** of Sickness	16	*17*
The **Shift** in Perception	16	*17*
HOW are Healing and Atonement Related?	53	*55*
HOW is **Judgment** Relinquished?	26	*27*
HOW Do God's Teachers Deal with **Magic Thoughts**?	42	*44*
HOW Can Perception of **Order of Difficulties** Be Avoided?	23	*24*
HOW Is **Peace** Possible in This World?	28	*29*
HOW Should the Teacher of God **Spend His Day**?	38	*40*
HOW Will the **World End**?	35	*36*
HOW MANY Teachers of God...Needed to **Save the World**?	30	*31*
INTRODUCTION	1	*1*
Does **JESUS** Have a Special Place in Healing?	55	*58*
Is Each One to **Be JUDGED** in the End?	37	*·38*

Second Edition numbers in *italics*

ADDITIONS / NOTES

How is **JUDGMENT** Relinquished?......................................26   *27*
What Is **JUSTICE**?..47   *49*
What Are the **LEVELS** of Teaching?..................................6   *7*
How Do God's Teachers Deal with **MAGIC THOUGHTS**?....42   *44*
How Can Perception of **ORDER of DIFFICULTIES** Be Avoided?. 23   *24*
How Is **PEACE** Possible in This World?..............................28   *29*
What Is the **PEACE of GOD**?..49   *51*
Are "**PSYCHIC**" **POWERS** Desirable?..............................59   *62*
Who Are Their **PUPILS**?...4   *5*
Is **REINCARNATION** So?..57   *60*
What Is the **RESURRECTION**?..65   *68*
What Is the Real Meaning of **SACRIFICE**?........................32   *33*
How many Teachers of God..Needed to **SAVE the WORLD**?...30   *31*
How Should the Teacher of God **SPEND HIS DAY**?..............38   *40*
Who Are **God's TEACHERS**?..3   *3*
WHAT Are the **Characteristics** of God's Teachers?...............8   *9*
WHAT Is **Death**?..63   *66*
WHAT Is **Justice**?...47   *49*
WHAT Are the **Levels** of Teaching?.....................................6   *7*
WHAT Is the **Peace of God**?..49   *51*
WHAT Is the **Resurrection**?..65   *68*
WHAT Is the Real Meaning of **Sacrifice**?..........................32   *33*
WHAT Is the Role of **WORDS** in Healing?..........................51   *53*
WHO Are Their **Pupils**?..4   *5*
WHO are **God's Teachers**?...3   *3*
How Will the **WORLD** End?..35   *36*
............**AS FOR THE REST** 67   *70*

CLARIFICATION OF TERMS
ALPHABETICAL

                                            Page *Page*
The **EGO** - The Miracle 77   *81*
EPILOGUE 87   *91*
FORGIVENESS - The Face of Christ 79   *83*
The **HOLY SPIRIT** 85   *89*
INTRODUCTION 73   *77*
JESUS - Christ...83   *87*
MIND - Spirit 75   *79*
TRUE PERCEPTION - Knowledge 81   *85*

Second Edition numbers in *italics*

Additional copies of this Index may be obtained
from your favorite bookseller
or
by sending a check or money order for $10.00 per
copy (includes shipping and handling) to:

Indexing Miracles Group
P.O. Box 3441
Brentwood, TN 37027